P9-EIE-197

INSIDER'S GUIDE TO THE BODY

# The Nervous System

**Walter Oleksy**

the rosen publishing group's
rosen central

Published in 2001 by The Rosen Publishing Group, Inc.
29 East 21st Street, New York, NY 10010

**Library of Congress Cataloging-in-Publication Data**

Oleksy, Walter G., 1930–
  The nervous system / by Walter Oleksy. — 1st ed.
      p. cm. — (Insider's guide to the body)
Includes bibliographical references and index.
  ISBN 0-8239-3341-5 (lib. bdg.)
   1.  Nervous system—Juvenile literature. 2. Nervous system—Diseases—Juvenile literature. [1. Nervous system.]  I. Title. II. Series.
  QP361.5 .O44 2000
  612.8—dc21
                                              00-009381

*Manufactured in the United States of America*

# Contents

# 1

# You and Your Body

Do you know how you're able to walk to school and run in the playground? Do you know how you are able to taste pizza and smell flowers? How about reading books and writing school reports? Or how about playing soccer or a computer game? Do you know how your body is able to do all of the wonderful things it is able to do? You might be surprised to find out that it's all because of your body's nervous system.

## Two Systems of the Body

Your body actually has two communication systems that control its functions and actions. These are the nervous system and the endocrine system. The nervous system sends messages from your brain through your body in the form of nerve signals to make it do certain things, like raising your hand in class or kicking a ball. The endocrine system sends messages in the form of body chemicals called hormones. Hormones are then carried by blood and spread through your body to activate the functions of specific body parts.

Testosterone, shown here through an electron microscope, is a hormone that affects male sexual development. The release of hormones is controlled by the endocrine system.

The nervous system is the body's complex information gatherer, storage center, and control system. It makes sure that all of your body's parts are working together efficiently. It controls and coordinates all the activities of your body: everything you do, see, hear, feel, smell, or touch. It is responsible for your thoughts, emotions, and memory. It also controls your body temperature, balance, and behavior.

# Take a Trip Through Your Body

When you go on a trip, your starting point is usually your home, right? Well, on a trip through your body, your starting point is your head—actually, the brain inside of your head. Your brain is your body's "home" because everything you do, feel, think, or say begins in your brain. Your brain accomplishes all of these things by sending messages to various parts of your body, commanding them to do their jobs. These messages travel through nerves down your spinal cord.

# The Funny Bone

Nerves are the communication system of your body. They carry messages to and from the brain and spinal cord. Here's an example: Remember the last time you hit your funny bone? It probably happened when you accidentally bumped your elbow against something. Then you felt a strange tingling sensation in your arm.

What you did was hit the nerve that passes below your elbow on its way to your forearm and hand. The physical shock to the nerve disturbed its normal functioning.

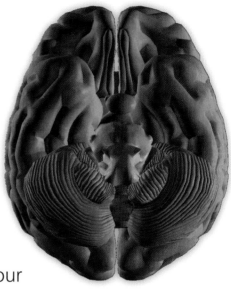

**A cross section of the brain showing its two symmetrical hemispheres**

The tingling sensation went away as soon as the nerve recovered from the shock. Nerve signals are electrical. But they are only about one-twentieth of a volt in power. Your spinal cord is like a network of nerves. The nerves travel down your neck and back and into your arms, legs, fingers, and toes. You can picture this by thinking of your brain and spinal cord as a big tree. The roots that extend from the tree into the ground are like the nerves branching out from your spinal cord. These nerves keep branching off from each other as they travel to different parts of your body.

# The Nervous System: Great Scientific Discoveries

More than 2,000 years ago, doctors and scientists began studying the human nervous system. In 400 BC, Hippocrates, a Greek doctor, argued that the brain had the power of thought and understanding. In AD 160, Galen, a Greek anatomist, showed that the brain sent messages to the body through the spinal cord. But he thought it was because an animal spirit in liquid form passed through the body or mind.

This neuron is located in the brain's gray matter near the spinal cord.

In 1543, Andreas Vesalius, a Belgian anatomist, demonstrated that thoughts and feelings originated in the brain. A seventeenth-century Dutch scientist, Jan Swammerdam, discovered that muscles cause movement by contracting rather than expanding.

A century later, in the 1770s, Luigi Galvani, an Italian anatomist, found that electricity causes muscles to contract. In the 1790s, German doctor Franz Gull maintained that various parts of the brain controlled various parts of the body.

In 1873, an Italian doctor, Camillo Golgi, was the first to observe nerve cells. It happened when he used a special stain that darkened the neurons, allowing them to be more easily seen under a microscope. In the late 1800s, a German scientist, Walther Nernst, discovered that messages were carried along nerves by electrochemical reactions.

In the early 1950s, British scientists Alan Lloyd Hodgkin and Andrew Fielding Huxley showed how nerve messages are transmitted to the brain. In 1970, Julius Axelrod of the United States, Ulf von Euler of Sweden, and Bernard Katz of Great Britain shared a Nobel Prize for research into the mechanisms of nerve transmission.

In 1975, Scottish scientist John Hughes and Hans Kosterlitz discovered endorphins, which are natural brain chemicals with painkilling effects. In 1986, Stanley Cohen of the United States and Rita Levi-Montalcini of Italy shared a Nobel Prize for the discovery of nerve-growth factors. Research to find ways to relieve nervous system disorders and pain continues to be conducted by renowned scientists all over the world.

## Fun Facts and Figures

Bet you never knew the following things about your nervous system:

- Your brain weighs about 2.75 pounds (1.25 kg). That is about 2 percent of your total body weight.

- There are about 100 billion nerve cells, or neurons, in your brain.

- Most neurons are connected to at least 50,000 others. Some are linked to five times that number.

- Over three-quarters of your brain and spinal cord are made up of water.

- Your brain is a fantastic memory storehouse. It holds more than 1,000 times the information in a twenty-volume encyclopedia.

- Your brain works twenty-four hours a day to keep your body running smoothly—even while you sleep.

- An adult's spinal cord is about 17.5 inches (45 cm) long. It weighs only about 1 ounce (30 g).

- Thirty-one pairs of spinal nerves branch out from your spinal cord.

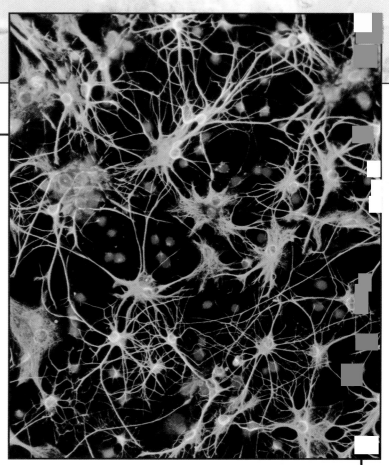

**Brain cells from the cortex region**

- Bone cells have a life span of twenty years. Skin cells live for only three weeks.

- Your body has more than 600 skeletal muscles. In adults, muscles make up nearly half of the body's weight.

- About 30,000 miles (50,000 km) of nerves snake through your body.

# 2

# Your Nervous System

Now that you know some background, are you ready to take a trip through your nervous system? Your body doesn't have just one nervous system. It has four nervous systems: the central nervous system, the peripheral nervous system, the somatic nervous system, and the autonomic nervous system.

The central nervous system consists of the brain and the spinal cord. The central nervous system is like a main switchboard that controls and coordinates the activities of the entire nervous system. It analyzes information, stores it, and issues instructions to the body.

## Nerves

Your body has both motor and sensory fibers that are bound together in bundles called nerves. Your nervous system contains about 30,000 miles (50,000 km) of nerves. They wind their way from your head to your toes and fingers.

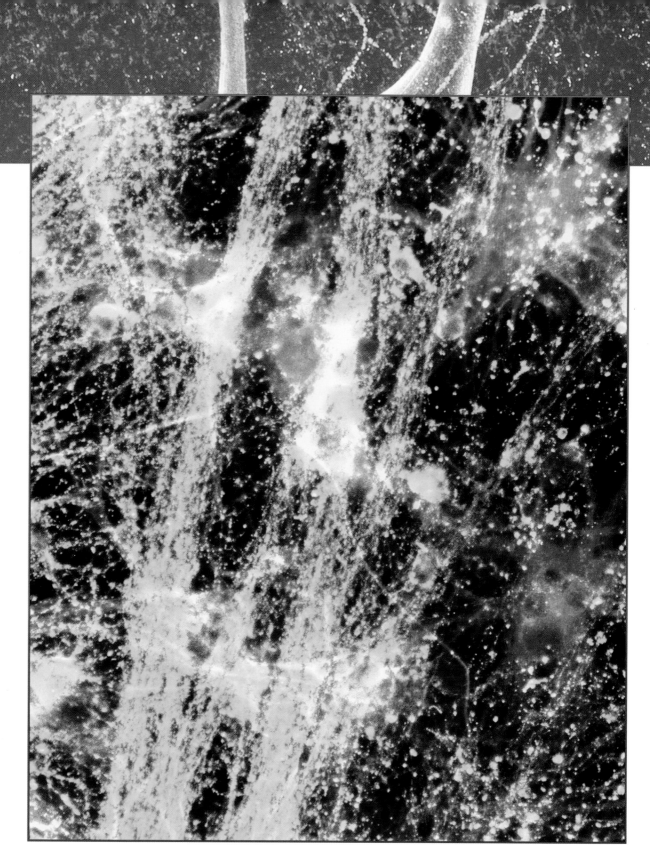

This network of neurons in the cerebral cortex allows for the transmission of nerve impulses.

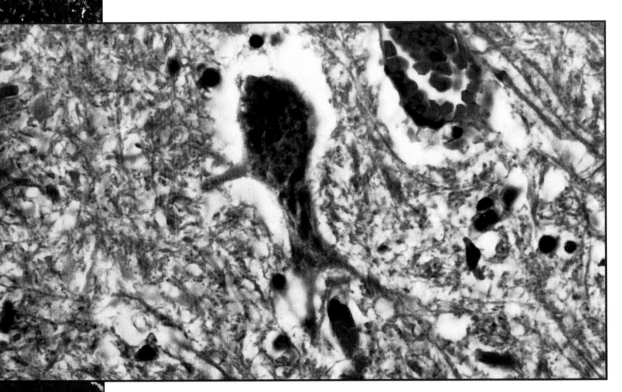

**The neurons in the cerebral cortex are responsible for the basic functions of the human brain.**

The network of nerves radiating outward from your spinal cord is called the outer, or peripheral, nervous system. Thirty-one pairs of nerves leave the spinal cord through openings between the vertebrae. These nerves carry "two-way traffic"—both motor and sensory nerve fibers from the root of the spinal cord. The sensory fibers of the peripheral nervous system extend to the skin, muscles, joints, and various sense organs. The motor fibers go to muscles, glands, and blood vessels.

The peripheral nervous system is divided into two parts: an outer system called the somatic (body) system and an inner one called the autonomic system.

The peripheral nervous system is made up of all the nerve tissue outside the central nervous system, that is, the brain and spinal cord itself. There are also twelve pairs of cranial nerves. They originate in the brain and control speech and sight, as well as movement of the neck, larynx, and tongue. They are also considered part of the peripheral nervous system.

# The Somatic Nervous System

The somatic nervous system controls voluntary actions. It springs into action whenever you make a conscious movement. It carries messages to your muscles and makes them contract.

The somatic nervous system has two responsibilities. It collects information from your body's sense organs. It then sends this information along sensory nerve fibers to the central nervous system. It also carries signals from the central nervous system to the muscles along motor nerve fibers.

# The Autonomic Nervous System

The term "autonomic" means self-controlled and independent of outside influences. The autonomic nervous system controls the automatic functions of your body: the activities that keep operating in your body that you never think about, like breathing, your heartbeat, and the passage of food and liquids. These parts of your body

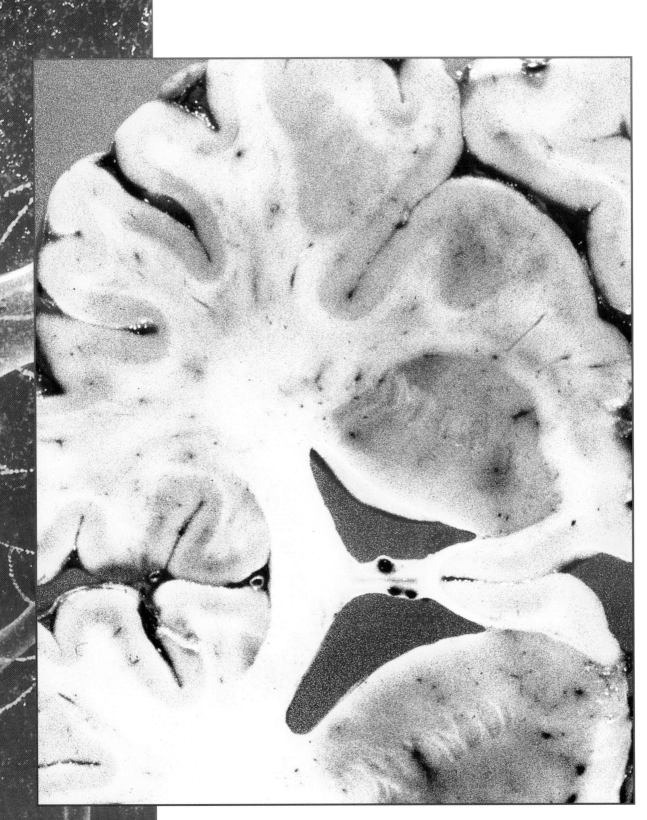

This is a cross section of the basal ganglia, a tissue mass that contains nerve-cell bodies and connects to the central nervous system.

function without your awareness. For that reason, the autonomic nervous system is also called the involuntary nervous system or "the system that never sleeps."

The autonomic system has two divisions: the sympathetic and the parasympathetic. Both systems contain masses of tissue containing nerve-cell bodies called ganglia. They connect the central nervous system and the body structure served by the autonomic system.

The two divisions of the autonomic system act in opposite ways on each organ of the body. The sympathetic division speeds up body activities, while the parasympathetic division slows them down. For example, the sympathetic system speeds up your heartbeat, and the parasympathetic system slows it down.

# 3

# The Brain

Your brain is like a computer. It holds millions of bits of information. If you think computers are smart, you'd be surprised to find out that your brain is even smarter. It has to be. It is your body's "control center." It tells all of your body parts what to do. Your brain works twenty-four hours a day to keep your mind and body running smoothly. It keeps your heart beating and your lungs breathing. Your brain keeps all of your body systems working efficiently.

The nervous system connects your entire body with its master control center—the brain. Sensory nerves carry messages from your sense organs to your brain. Your brain processes this information and sends messages to your muscles along motor nerves.

## Facts About the Brain

The brain is the largest and most complex part of the nervous system. It is a soft, grayish pink, jellylike organ. It is about the size of a large grapefruit and weighs about three pounds (1.4 kg). Your brain

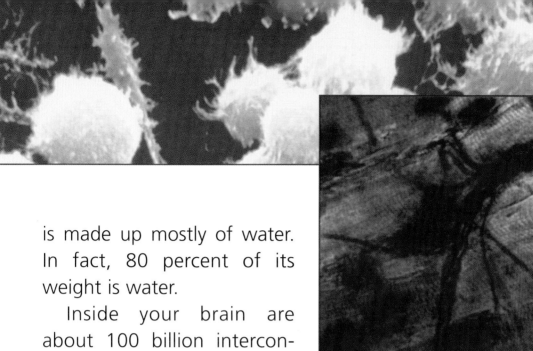

is made up mostly of water. In fact, 80 percent of its weight is water.

Inside your brain are about 100 billion interconnecting, microscopic, building-block nerve cells called neurons. Neurons are highly specialized bundles of cells that send impulses (one-way electrochemical messages) to and from the brain and spinal cord. The messages are sent faster than you can blink your eyes.

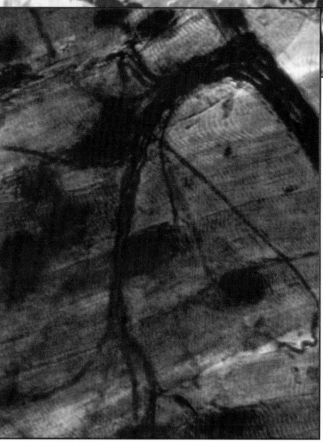

**Brain tissue contains more than 100 billion interconnected neurons.**

A neuron is made up of a cell body, which contains a nucleus, fine, threadlike branches called dendrites, and a wirelike axon. Dendrites are short fibers that carry messages in the form of electrical impulses to the cell body. The word "dendrite" comes from the Greek word *dendron*, meaning "tree." Dendrites are branching, tubelike extensions of the cell body that form a pattern that resembles the limbs of a tree.

One long nerve fiber, the axon, carries messages away from the cell body to the dendrites of other neurons. Axons are finer than a hair but may be more than three feet (1 m) long. Peripheral nerves are made up of bundles of axons.

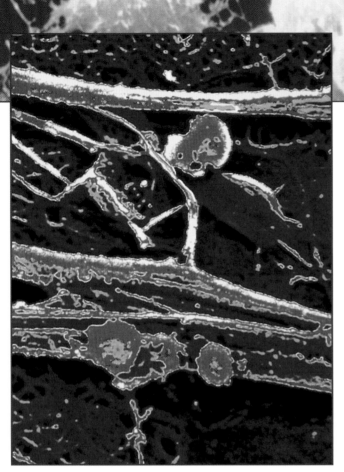

**Axons transmit nerve impulses.**

Your brain sends messages to parts of the body through the nerves at speeds as fast as 250 miles per hour. The neurons pick up signals from one part of the nervous system and carry them to another. The signals are then passed on to other neurons to bring about some action.

A nerve is actually a lot of nerve fibers (axons, dendrites, or both) that are bound together. Each nerve cell has a body and a long fiber attached to it. Damaged fibers can regrow, but if the body of the cell is damaged, it cannot be replaced.

# A Knee-Jerk Reaction

Want to see how messages travel to and from the brain? Try this experiment. It won't hurt, and it's fun. Sit in a chair and cross your legs. Ask someone to gently tap the tendon just below your kneecap. The tap stretches that muscle, an action that stimulates special receptors to produce an impulse. Your foot jerks up instantly. This is an example of a reflex action. It is something you do without thinking.

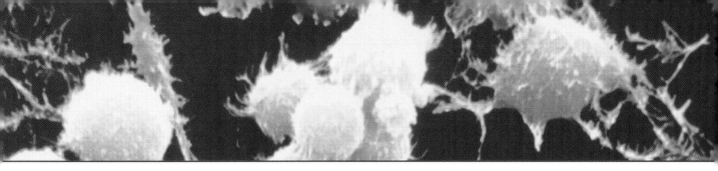

Now have your friend ask you to uncross your legs. This takes longer than the knee jerk because your brain has to process your friend's request. The request goes from your ears to your brain. The command then travels from your brain by way of nerve cells to the leg muscles that are being uncrossed.

# Dissecting the Brain

Your brain is divided into three main sections: the forebrain, the midbrain, and the hindbrain. The brain has three main structural parts: the cerebrum, the cerebellum, and the brain stem. Each part controls certain functions.

# The Forebrain

The cerebrum is the largest part of the brain. It accounts for about four-fifths of the brain's total weight. It makes up most of the forebrain and between 85 and 90 percent of the whole human brain. The cerebrum controls most of the brain's work. The centers that enable you to see, hear, taste, smell, touch, think, remember, and make decisions and that govern your body muscles are all found in the outermost layer of the cerebrum—the cerebral cortex.

*Cortex* is a Latin word for "bark," like the bark of a tree. It is a thin sheet of tissue that makes up the outer layer of the brain. Some functions of the cortex include thought, voluntary movement, language, reasoning, and perception. A voluntary movement or action is one that you are aware of and can start or stop at will, such as walking,

running, eating, and reading. Voluntary actions are controlled by nerves that send messages to the body's skeletal muscles.

Different parts of the cerebrum both send and receive messages from various parts of the body. Some parts get messages from your eyes and ears so you can see and hear. Some parts of the cerebrum control your muscle movements. Other parts enable you to learn and remember things.

## The Limbic System

Between the two halves of the cerebrum lie the two most important parts of the forebrain: the thalamus and the hypothalamus. They are parts of what is called the brain's limbic system. They control the emotional response you have to a given situation. The thalamus is the brain's main "relay station." It controls sensory and motor integration by sending information to and from the cerebral cortex.

The hypothalamus is about the size of a pea and is located at the base of the brain. It is like a thermostat because it controls your body temperature. It also controls your emotions, as well as feelings of hunger and thirst. Another part of the limbic system is the hippocampus. It controls your memory and ability to learn.

## The Midbrain

The midbrain includes structures whose functions include vision, hearing, and eye and body movements. The midbrain and some of the hindbrain make up the brain stem. The brain stem is the area of the brain that connects the cerebrum with the spinal cord. The brain stem controls all the basic functions of your body. It keeps your lungs breathing, your heart beating, and your blood pressure stable—all without you even thinking about it.

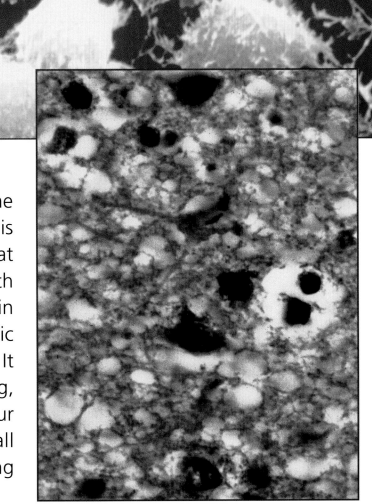

These neurons are located in the spinal cord.

# The Hindbrain

The hindbrain is divided into three parts: pons, medulla oblongata, and cerebellum. The pons is the point where nerve fibers from the body join to cross into the upper parts of the brain. The medulla oblongata is the lowest part of the brain stem and leads to the spinal cord. The medulla is responsible for controlling those vital tasks we take for granted—our heartbeat, breathing, digestion, and blood pressure.

The cerebellum is located in the rear of the skull. It is the unconscious motor-coordination center of the brain. It controls your body's movement and helps maintain its balance and posture. It

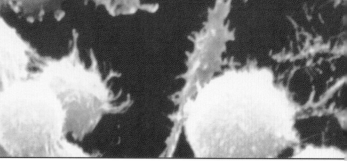

**A view of a cerebral hemisphere**

also coordinates complicated muscle movements, such as slam-dunking a basketball or flying a jet plane.

# Head and Brain Protection

The brain and spinal cord are the most important and best protected parts of the human body. The brain is covered by the skull, or cranium, which is a rigid helmet formed from twenty-nine hard, tough cranial bones that are tightly joined together.

The brain is also protected by three layers of membranes called the meninges. They cover the brain and cushion it against sudden knocks or vibrations. If you fall, hurt your head, or get hit by something, you can injure part of your brain. That's why bike riders and skateboard riders, among other athletes, wear helmets—to protect themselves against head injuries. An injury to any part of the brain could interfere with certain body functions. For instance, if you injure the part of the brain that controls seeing (the midbrain), you might lose your eyesight.

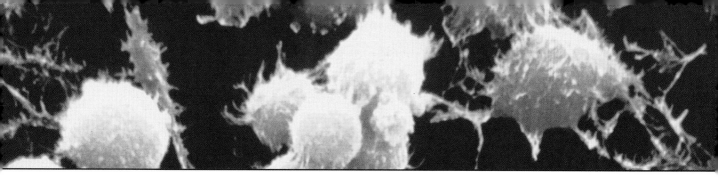

The spinal cord is covered by a flexible column of bones called vertebrae. The human body has thirty-three vertebrae. Vertebrae are rings of bone that fit snugly into one another. But they are flexible so you can bend and turn. The spinal cord is also suspended loosely in the vertebral canal, a position that keeps it from being hurt when the spinal column bends and twists.

There are two hemispheres, or sides, of the brain. We will learn about them in the next chapter and find out which side of your brain dominates how you think and feel.

**The brain is protected by three layers of membranes as well as the skull.**

# 4

# Two Sides of Your Brain

Your brain has two sides, or hemispheres—a left side and a right side. Each side controls different areas of your body. The right side of your brain controls the left side of your body. The left side of your brain controls the right side of your body. As your brain develops, one side of your brain becomes more dominant than the other and that affects how well you do certain things, making you better at sports than playing the piano, for example.

The side of your brain that is most developed also controls how good you are in doing things with your left or right hand. If the left side of your brain is more developed than the right side, you will be right-handed. If the right side of your brain is better developed, you will be left-handed. Your brain determined whether you would be right- or left-handed by the time you were three years old. About nine out of ten people are right-handed.

## The Left Side of the Brain

Left-brained people are more logical and strive for completion rather than creativity. They will be ordered, reasonable, and have good

**The two hemispheres of the brain, right and left, are each responsible for different areas and functions of the body.**

reading, writing, and verbal skills. They tend to test well in school and are good at solving difficult arithmetic problems.

# The Right Side of the Brain

Right-brained people are more visually oriented and creative, tending to be very good in the fine arts. They tend to have better rhythm, intuition, and a more vivid imagination than do left-brained people.

# Right Brain/Left Brain in School

Students whose right side of the brain is dominant may not score as highly on standard school tests as do their classmates who are left-brain dominant. They may even be considered slow learners. In recent years, educators have been considering new tests for right-brained students. Right-brained students are just as smart as left-brained students; they just process information differently.

# Which Side of Your Brain Is Dominant?

● If you can express your feelings easily, you're probably right-brained. If not, you're probably left-brained.

● If you prefer classes where you have only one assignment at a time, you're probably left-brained. If you can study many things at once, you're probably right-brained.

● If you prefer multiple-choice tests, you're probably right-brained. If you prefer essay exams, you're probably left-brained.

● If you're good at thinking up funny things to say or do, you're probably right-brained. If not, you're probably left-brained.

● If you like to know exactly what you are supposed to do, you're probably left-brained. If you are open and flexible, you're probably right-brained.

● If you're inventive, you're probably right-brained. If you're only occasionally inventive, you're probably left-brained.

● If you like clear and immediate applications, such as mechanical drawing or home economics, you're probably right-brained. If you prefer work that does not have a clearly practical application, such as literature or history, you're probably left-brained.

● If you prefer to learn details and specific facts, you're probably left-brained. If you prefer a general overview of a subject, you are probably right-brained.

● If you are easily lost, you're probably left-brained. If you have a good sense of direction, you're probably right-brained.

● If you like to be in noisy places where lots of things are happening, you're probably right-brained. If you like to be where you can concentrate on one thing to your best ability, you are probably left-brained.

Of course, both sides of your brain are interactive. Determining which side of your brain is dominant is not an exact science. The brain still holds many mysteries that are waiting to be discovered. Now let's learn more about the spinal cord, a vital part of your nervous system.

# 5

# The Spinal Cord

Your spinal cord is a downward extension of your brain. It is like a long, cream-colored string that starts at the bottom of your brain and extends all the way down your back. Nerves branch off from your spinal cord and reach down your toes and through your fingers. Some sections of the spinal cord are as thick as a rope, but others are as thin and narrow as a single strand of hair. In adult women, the spinal cord is about 16 inches (43 cm) long. In adult men, it is about 17 inches (45 cm) long. It weighs between 1.2 to 1.4 ounces (35–40 g).

The spinal cord is shielded by other body parts, including muscles. It is located inside a long channel of bones called the vertebral column, or backbone. The thirty-three rings of bone that make up the vertebral column fit tightly into one another. But even though the bones, or vertebrae, fit together snugly, they still let you bend and turn with ease. You can feel your vertebrae if you run your fingers down your back. Each spinal bone contains a hole. Each bone's hole is lined up to form a tube that houses the spinal cord and main nerves.

**The spinal cord is loosely suspended within a flexible column of thirty-three vertebrae, which allows the body to bend and twist.**

There are many nerves that branch out along the spinal cord and travel to various parts of your body. They are called spinal nerves. Information travels through these nerves both to and from the spinal column. The messages tell your brain or parts of your body what to do. The messages that are put into motion are called reflexes.

# Reflex Activity

The term "reflex" comes from the word "reflect," which means to turn back. Reflex actions are the nervous system's quick responses to possible danger or harm to your body. For example, when you touch something hot, your hand pulls away quickly. That is what is known as a reflex action.

Most reflex actions are automatic responses controlled by your spinal cord. This is how a reflex happens: In the case of touching something hot, the sense organ in your finger or hand detected the dangerous heat and sent nerve signals up your spinal cord to your brain. From there, the brain sent signals to the muscles that made you pull your hand away.

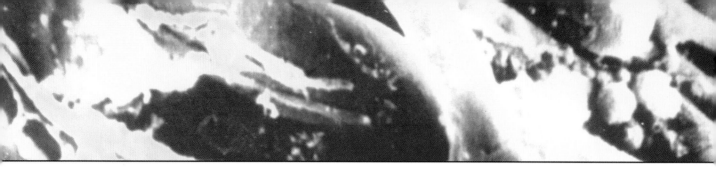

# Reflex Arcs

Messages to and from the brain pass through the spinal nerves by means of what is called a reflex arc. A reflex arc involves the stimulation of a receptor. Receptors are specialized neurons that are located in the ears, eyes, and other sense organs.

For example, if you walk barefoot and step on a stone, the reflex arc stimulation would come from a pain receptor in your toe. That triggers an impulse that travels up a sensory nerve to your spinal cord. From there, the impulse meets up with a connecting neuron. A connection is then made with motor neurons, which start muscle contractions that pull your foot up and off the stone. All this happens in the blink of an eye. Nerve impulses travel along nerve fibers at lightning-fast speeds. Speeds range from 3 to 300 feet (.09 to 90 m) per second. The reflex arc is made up of three kinds of neurons (cells). They are the sensory, motor, and connector neurons. Sensory neurons are nerve cells that carry messages to the brain or spinal cord. Motor neurons are nerve cells that carry messages from the brain or spinal cord. Connector neurons are nerve cells in the brain or spinal cord that bind two other neurons together.

Let's return to the example of touching something hot. As soon as you touched it, very sensitive nerve cells in the skin of your hand sent out messages that recognized the pain you felt. The messages traveled along a sensory neuron to your spinal cord. There, a connector neuron made a connection with motor neurons that run to the muscles in the arm that was pulled away from

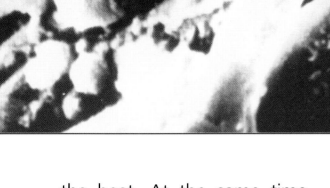

the heat. At the same time, other connector neurons flashed pain messages to your brain. Your brain instantly told you that you had touched something hot.

Your nervous system did not only cause you to remove your hand from the hot metal, it sent a sensation of pain up your spinal cord to your brain where it was processed as memory. That way, you will be reminded not to touch a hot pot handle in the future.

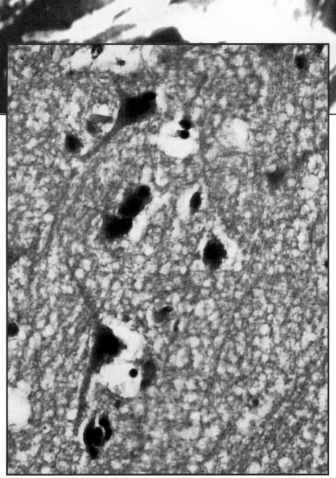

**Neurons in the spinal cord send important messages to the brain, which in turn tells the body how to respond.**

# 6

# Disorders of the Nervous System

When you are born, your nervous system is usually healthy. If you're careful, it will stay healthy all or most of your life. But things can happen to make it unhealthy. Accidents and misuse of drugs may injure parts of the nervous system. As you grow older, disease or viruses can also attack your nervous system.

## Head Injuries

Head injuries are a common cause of damage to the nervous system. That is why it is important to protect your head from falls and getting hit by anything, such as a baseball or bat.

Head injuries, which can cause physical and/or mental damage, are fairly common in young people because they are so active in play. About one in ten children lose consciousness as a result of a head injury. More than 500,000 children are hospitalized each year after suffering a head injury. Fortunately, most head injuries are minor and can be treated with an overnight stay in a hospital. More serious head injuries take longer to heal and may permanently affect our bodies and minds. Falls are the most common cause of head injuries in children under the age of ten. Car and motorcycle accidents are responsible for most head injuries during the teenage years.

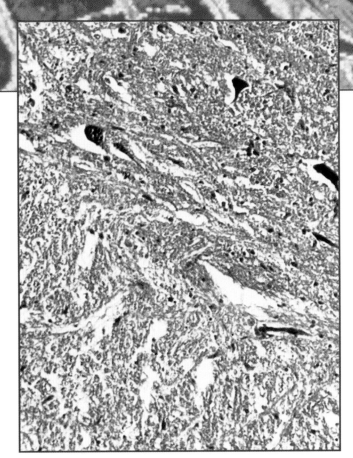

Blastomycosis, a disease caused by parasitic fungus, is destroying the nerve tissue in this spinal cord.

# Damage to the Nervous System

The billions of neurons that make up the central nervous system can wear out or be damaged by accidents and disorders. Bacteria and viruses can cause acute infections of the nervous system. As people grow older, many of their neurons simply wear out. The branch of medicine that deals with diseases of the nervous system—affecting the brain, spinal cord, and nerves of the body—is called neurology.

Damage and inflammation of the neurons can cause pain along the path of a nerve. The resulting disorders are called neuritis and neuralgia. The pain can be treated to some extent with medication.

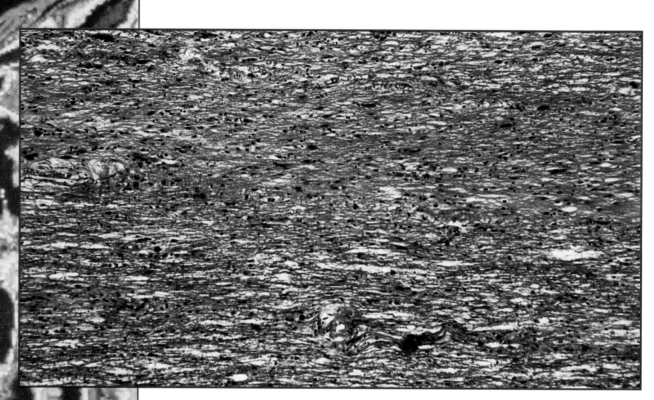

**The spongy appearance of nerve tissue in this spinal cord is due to the loss of the myelin sheath of axons, a common sign of multiple sclerosis.**

One of the most common disorders of the nervous system is a stroke. That is what happens when the supply of blood to part of the brain is blocked off. Neurons in the brain die quickly, affecting some of the body's functions such as speech, sight, and movement. Other cells in the brain are sometimes able to take control of these functions.

Other problems in the nervous system are caused by injuries. Damage to the brain at birth can cause cerebral palsy and spastic paralysis. Damage to the spinal cord can also cause paralysis in which there is no feeling in the arms, legs, or other parts of the body.

Besides accidents and viruses, smoking and drug abuse can also lead to disorders of the nervous system.

Heavy drinking of alcoholic beverages can speed up the rate at which nerve cells in the brain die.

Symptoms of nervous system disorders are numbness, dizziness, and loss of balance or physical coordination. Persons suffering from any of these symptoms should consult their doctor. Other disorders of the nervous system include Alzheimer's disease, causing memory loss; encephalitis, which causes excessive sleepiness and is sometimes called "sleeping sickness"; meningitis, causing paralysis; multiple sclerosis (MS), causing nerve fibers to lose their ability to function properly; Parkinson's disease, causing loss of mental and motion capabilities; and poliomyelitis (infantile paralysis), causing paralysis. To treat nervous system disorders, doctors may prescribe antibiotics, radiation and vitamin therapy, or recommend surgery.

# How Other Cultures Treat Spinal Cord Disorders

For thousands of years, many Asian and Eastern countries such as China and Russia have treated spinal cord disorders in natural ways that are only now gaining wider acceptance in Western nations. Instead of medication or surgery, they put pressure on or otherwise manipulate the spinal column with needles or their hands. These treatments include chiropractic medicine, acupuncture, and acupressure.

Chiropractic medicine is a medical practice based on the theory that all disease results from a disruption of the function of the nerves. The main interference is believed to be caused by a misaligned vertebra, which blocks the life force that flows from the brain down the

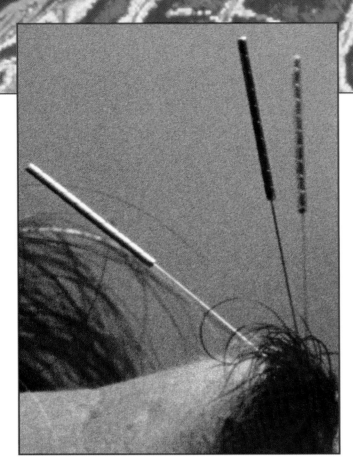

**Acupuncture, a traditional Chinese needle therapy, is believed to stimulate the autonomic nervous system.**

spinal cord to various parts of the body, and adjusting the vertebra is thought to restore good health. This is mainly done by massage and manipulation of the vertebra by hand.

Chiropractic medicine has been practiced in the United States and other Western countries since the late 1800s and has been considered a controversial medical treatment from the very beginning. Gradually, however, it has gained recognition as an accepted medical practice.

Acupuncture is a traditional Chinese medical treatment in which needles are inserted into the skin at specific pressure points. In 1974, the United States' National Institutes of Health approved the study of acupuncture for the possible relief of arthritis and other pain. It is believed that acupuncture works by stimulating or repressing the autonomic nervous system in various ways.

Acupressure is a form of acupuncture that does not involve the use of needles. It is similar to a massage in that it relies on the use of the fingers and hands to press key points on the skin's surface. This action allows the body's immune system to self-heal.

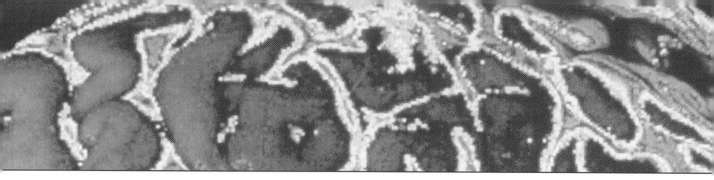

# Cutting-Edge Technology and Medical Breakthroughs

A fall can cause serious injury to the head and spinal column, causing paralysis—the inability to move your arms or legs. About 250,000 Americans suffer from paralysis due to spinal cord injuries. Each year, some 10,000 people become victims, as a result of disease, accidents, or sports injuries. In 1995, Christopher Reeve, the actor who played Superman in the movies, became paralyzed when he fell from his horse during a competition. He landed on his head and instantly became a quadriplegic. He survived an operation that reattached his head to his spinal cord, but he could no longer walk or use his arms. Reeve has since become an advocate for spinal cord injury research. He and thousands of others with similar injuries are hopeful about ongoing research into spinal cord regeneration. The research involves experiments using antibodies and nerve growth factors.

The main challenge for spinal cord researchers is to get damaged nerves to reconnect. Rebuilding nerve networks to carry sensations of pain and relief would enable paralysis victims to regain at least some use of their arms and legs. "For a hundred years, the belief was that the adult nervous system does not regenerate," said Dr. Fred Gage, a neuroscientist with the Salk Institute for Biological Studies. "But now we know that is not true. There has been tremendous progress in the regeneration of the spinal cord. I am confident that in his lifetime, Chris [Reeve] will be exposed to treatment that will have some significant effect on the quality of his life."

# Glossary

**autonomic nervous system**   Nerves that carry out various automatic functions, such as breathing.

**axon**   Long fiber that sends signals from a nerve-cell body.

**brain**   Central controlling and coordinating organ of the nervous system.

**brain stem**   Lower part of the brain.

**central nervous system**   The brain and spinal cord.

**cerebellum**   Part of the brain that coordinates balance and movement.

**cerebrum**   Part of the brain that controls thought, feeling, memory, and muscle movement.

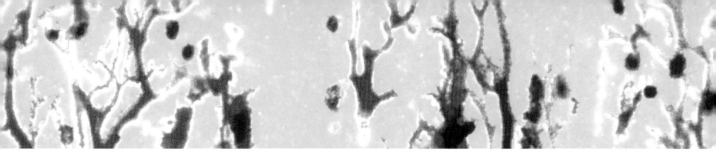

**contraction**   The action of squeezing together.

**dendrite**   Tiny fiber that carries signals to a nerve cell.

**fiber**   Thin, threadlike structure.

**ganglia**   Masses of nerve cells bunched together.

**heart**   Major organ that pumps blood to the blood vessels of the body.

**limbic system**   Regions of the brain concerned with emotions.

**muscle**   Fibrous tissue that contracts (gets shorter) to produce movement.

**nerve cell**   Cell of the nervous system whose fibers send and receive impulses.

**nerve fibers**   Axons and dendrites.

**neuron**   A nerve cell.

**paralysis**   Loss of feeling or use of part of the body.

**peripheral nervous system**   Sensory and motor nerves that connect the brain and spinal cord to the rest of the body.

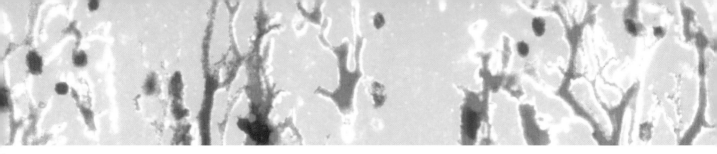

**pons**  Part of the brain stem.

**reflex actions**  Actions performed automatically.

**reflex arc**  Nerve pathway for a reflex action.

**spinal cord**  Long cord of nerves through the spine that connects the brain with the rest of the body.

**vertebrae**  Set of thirty-three bones that make up the spinal column.

# For More Information

## In the United States

Christopher Reeve Paralysis Foundation
500 Morris Avenue
Springfield, NJ 07081
(800) 225-0292
e-mail: info@crpf.org
Web site: http://www.paralysis.org

Miami Project to Cure Paralysis
P.O. Box 016960 (R-48)
Miami, FL 33101-6960
(800) STAND-UP
e-mail: mpinfo@miamiproject.med.miami.edu
Web site: http://www.miamiproject.miami.edu

## In Canada

Montréal Neurological Institute
3801 University Street

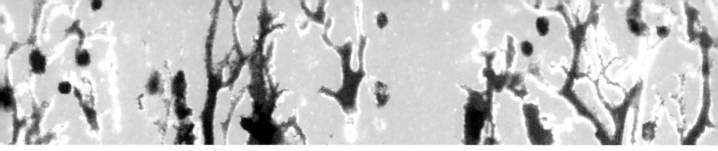

Montréal, PQ H3A 2B4
e-mail: director@mni.lan.mcgill.ca
Web site: http://www.mcgill.ca/mni

NeuroScience Canada Foundation
1650 Cedar Avenue, Suite 17-132
Montréal, PQ H3G 1A4
(514) 934-8408
e-mail: info@neurosciencefoundation.ca
Web site: http://www.neurosciencefoundation.ca/

# Web Sites

Acupressure.org
www.acupressure.org

Acupuncture.com
www.acupuncture.com

American Chiropractic Association
www.amerchiro.org

Health for Kids
www.kidshealth.about.com

SpineWire
www.spinewire.com

Virtual Hospital: The Central Nervous System
www.vh.org

# For Further Reading

Silverstein, Alvin, Virginia Silverstein, and Robert Silverstein. *The Nervous System.* New York: Twenty-First Century Books/Henry Holt, 1995.

Balkwill, Fran, and Mic Rolph. *The Incredible Human Body: A Book of Discovery and Learning.* Avenel, NJ: Sterling, 1996.

Haslam, Andrew, and Liz Wyze. *The Body* (Make It Work). Chicago, IL: World Book/Two-Can, 1998.

Parker, Steve. *The Brain and Nervous System.* New York: Raintree Steck-Vaughn, 1997.

Parrott, Robert H. *Your Wonderful Body!* Washington, DC: National Geographic Society, 1994.

Stille, Darlene R. *The Nervous System.* Danbury, CT: Children's Press, 1997.

Ward, Alan. *Experimenting with Science: About Yourself.* New York: Chelsea House, 1991.

# Index

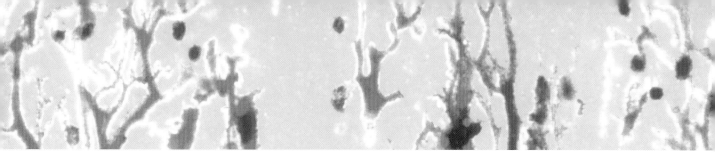

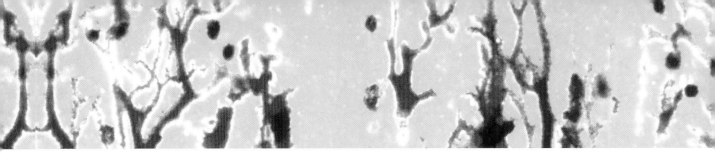

## About the Author

Walter Oleksy writes on science, careers, and other subjects for young readers. Oleksy lives in a Chicago suburb with his dog, Max. To learn more about Walter's books, go to *http://home.earthlink.net/~waltmax/bio.html*.

## Photo Credits

Pp. 5, 24, 36, 38 © Custom Medical; pp. 7, 25, 27, 28-29, 31 © Life Art; pp. 16, 20 © Jan Leestma, M.D./Custom Medical; p. 8 © Jan Leestma, M.D./Science Photo Library (SPL)/Photo Researchers, Inc.; pp. 11, 13 © Nancy Kedersha/UCLA/Science Photo Library/Custom Medical; pp. 14, 23, 33 © Keith/Custom Medical; p. 19 © Corbis; p. 35 © Astrid & Hanns-Frieder Michler/SPL/Photo Researchers, Inc.

Cover, front matter, and back matter © Alfred Pasicka/SPL/Photo Researchers, Inc.: Nerve cells in the cerebellum.
Chapter 1 © Jan Leestma, M.D./Custom Medical: neuroblasts.
Chapter 2 © Leonard D. Dank/Custom Medical: a neuron synapse.
Chapter 3 © David M. Phillips/Photo Researchers, Inc: chemical neurotransmitters.
Chapter 4 © Corbis: neurons in the spinal cord.
Chapter 5 © Corbis: spinal cord tissue.
Chapter 6 © Martin/Custom Medical: nerve cells in the cerebral cortex.

## Layout

Geri Giordano

## Series Design

Cindy Williamson